WiderWorld

POWERED BY

Practice
Tests Plus

EXAM PRACTICE
PEARSON TEST OF ENGLISH GENERAL **LEVEL 2**

Pearson Education Limited
Edinburgh Gate
Harlow
Essex CM20 2JE
and Associated Companies throughout the world.

Seventh impression 2020
First published 2016
ISBN: 9781292148854

Set in Arial
Printed and bound in Great Britain by Ashford Colour Press Ltd

Acknowledgements
Material for Test 1 and Test 2 taken from PTE General Skills Booster Level 2

Illustrations
Illustrated by Katerina Milusheva p. 21 and 39

Contents

Introduction

What is Pearson Test of English General?

PTE General is a suite of six tests at different levels (A1, 1, 2, 3, 4 and 5). It tests your ability in English in practical skills for real-life situations such as writing messages, understanding talks, understanding newspaper and magazine articles or taking part in conversations. PTE General tests are taken **three** times a year in May, June and December in centres all around the world.

The tests do not assume any experience of work or knowledge of the world and so are most suitable for teenagers and young adults who expect to use English in their future academic and professional lives.

Key Features

The sections and items in PTE General Level 2 are grouped together into themes or topics related to familiar and routine matters such as the home, the family, shopping, work, education, travel, entertainment. Most of the listening and reading texts are authentic and are taken from radio broadcasts, newspaper and magazine articles, telephone conversations, announcements, etc. The tests are international, so the reading and listening texts are taken from a range of English-speaking countries – the UK, the USA, Australia, etc. The four skills – listening, speaking, reading and writing – are tested in an integrated way. For example, you listen to some information and write about what you have heard, or you read a text and then answer questions or complete notes based on what you have read.

Test Structure

PTE General is divided into two parts – the Written Test and the Spoken Test.

The Written Test

The Written Test of PTE General consists of nine sections and takes 1 hour and 35 minutes at Level 2.

Section 1: Listening

Section 1 consists of ten short listening texts – dialogues or monologues. Each text is followed by a question and three possible answers. You must choose the correct answer by putting a cross (✗) in a box. There is a short pause before each recording for you to read the answers. This section tests your ability to understand the main idea of what someone says. You will hear the recording only once.

Section 2: Listening and Writing

Section 2 is a dictation. You will hear one person speaking and you must write down exactly what you hear with the correct spelling. You hear the recording twice, the second time with pauses to give you time to write. The passage can be a news broadcast, an announcement, instructions or factual information.

Section 3: Listening

In Section 3, you will hear two listening texts, either monologues or dialogues, and you have to complete notes for each listening using the information you have heard. There are five gaps to fill for each listening text. This section may test your ability to understand and write down detailed information including addresses, telephone numbers and website addresses. You will hear each text twice.

Section 4: Reading

In Section 4, you read five short texts, each containing a gap, and you choose which of three possible answers is the missing word or phrase that fills the gap. This section tests your ability to understand specific information and/or the overall meaning of the text. The reading texts can be instructions, signs, notices, advertisements, menus or announcements.

Section 5: Reading

Section 5 has one longer reading text. You read the text and answer five questions or complete five sentences from a choice of three possible answers. This section tests your understanding of the main idea of a text. The reading text can be a newspaper or magazine article, a leaflet, a brochure or a website article.

Section 6: Reading

There are two reading texts in this section. Each text is followed by four questions for you to answer using a word or a short phrase. They test your understanding of the main points of the texts. The types of reading can be articles from newspapers or magazines, leaflets, brochures or website articles.

Section 7: Reading

In Section 7, you read a text and use the information to fill in seven gaps in sentences or set of notes. This section tests your understanding of specific detailed information you have read. The reading text can be an email, letter, advertisement, newspaper or magazine article, or a section from a website or textbook.

Section 8: Writing

Section 8 is a writing test. You have to write a piece of correspondence – an email or a formal or informal letter – based on the information that you have read in Section 7. At Level 2, you have to write 70–90 words. In your letter or email, you are expected to ask for more information or to express your opinion on the subject. The topics in this section deal with things of everyday interest, including travel, the family, holidays, work, hobbies and current events.

Section 9: Writing

In Section 9, you will be asked to write a text from your own experience, knowledge or imagination. The text to write at Level 2 is 100–150 words long. You will be asked to write a text which gives your point of view, explains advantages and disadvantages, or develops an argument. There is a choice between two topics.

The Spoken Test

The Spoken Test of PTE General consists of four sections and takes 7 minutes at Level 2.

Section 10: Speaking

In the first part of the Test, the examiner will ask you a question and you have to talk about yourself for about a minute. You will talk about your interests, hobbies, the sports you take part in, the films or books you like, or about things you have done in the past. The examiner may ask you further questions to find out more information.

Section 11: Speaking

In Section 11, you will be asked to give your opinions and ideas about a subject suggested by the examiner, and to support your ideas. The examiner will take the opposite point of view for the discussion. The topics will include subjects of everyday interest, for example, the advantages of mobile phones, holidays at the beach or in the mountains, fast food, living in the city or in the country. The discussion will be for about 2 minutes.

Section 12: Speaking

In Section 12, you will be shown a picture and asked to describe it. First, you will be asked to describe what you can see in the picture and then you will be asked to describe one part of it in detail or to give your opinion about what is happening in the picture. You will have about 1.5 minutes to do this.

Section 13: Speaking

The final section of the Spoken Test is a role play. You will be given a card with details of your role, a situation and some instructions. The situation contains a problem which you have to solve by talking to the examiner, for example, making a complaint in a restaurant or refusing an invitation. This section of the Test takes about 2 minutes.

Exam Practice: PTE General

The *Exam Practice: PTE General* series has been specially written to help you become familiar with the format and content of the PTE General Test. The books contain two full practice tests, plus exam and writing guide sections to help you to improve your general level of English as well as your score in the test. Level 2 contains:

* Two *Practice Tests* for both the Written Test and the Spoken Test, the first of which has tips and strategies on how to approach the questions.

* A *Wordlist* with those words and phrases in the tests that you may need help with. Each item is followed by a definition.

* An *Exam Guide* with advice on how to approach each section and deal with particular problems that might occur.

* A *Writing Guide* which concentrates on the writing tasks you will meet in the tests, giving example answers, writing tips and useful language.

Practice Test 1 with Guidance

Section 1

You will have 10 seconds to read each question and the corresponding options. Then listen to the recording. After the recording you will have 10 seconds to choose the correct option. Put a cross (✗) in the box next to the correct answer, as in the example.

Example: Where is the man's passport?

A [✗] in his briefcase

B [ ] under the table

C [ ] in the car

1. What is Mandy doing?

   A [ ] working with Steve

   B [ ] apologising for not going to dinner

   C [ ] inviting a friend to dinner

2. Why is the speaker buying a card for his friend?

   A [ ] It's her birthday.

   B [ ] She likes flowers.

   C [ ] She helped him recently.

3. What is the relationship between Margaret and Pat?

   A [ ] They are cousins.

   B [ ] They are friends.

   C [ ] They are sisters.

4. What is the speaker's dad going to do?

   A [ ] baby-sit for Mary

   B [ ] take Alex to school

   C [ ] go to the dentist's

5. Where is the speaker?

A ☐ in London

B ☐ at a railway station

C ☐ on a train

6. Where are the speakers?

A ☐ at a travel agency

B ☐ at an airport

C ☐ at a restaurant

7. What kind of transport are the speakers talking about?

A ☐ a bicycle

B ☐ a bus

C ☐ a ferry

8. Who is talking to Mr Smith?

A ☐ a footballer

B ☐ a doctor

C ☐ a chemist

9. What is the woman looking for?

A ☐ a church

B ☐ a supermarket

C ☐ a sports centre

10. What does the boy want?

A ☐ a football shirt

B ☐ football boots

C ☐ trainers

Section 2

11. You will hear a recording about a sports competition. Listen to the whole recording once. Then you will hear the recording again with pauses for you to write down what you hear.
   Make sure you spell the words correctly.

Section 3

12–16 You will hear an announcement from a rail company. First, read the notes below, then listen and complete the notes with information from the announcement. You will hear the recording twice.

> **Example:** Announcement from: _Southern Trains_

12. Trains to London have been ....

13. Passengers can find buses to London ....

14. The expected delay to the London service is ....

15. Other services are ....

16. For more details go to ....

17–21 You will hear a recorded message. First, read the notes below, then listen and complete the notes with information from the recorded message. You will hear the recording twice.

> **Example:** Message for: _Janet_

17. Where son lives: ....

18. Reason for visit: ....

19. Length of stay in England: ....

20. Date of party: ....

21. Name of the restaurant: ....

Tip strip

14: The words "the expected delay … is" tell you that you are listening for a number.
18: Be careful. The woman mentions different possible reasons, but only one of them is correct.
19: Listen for the different things he will do in England. What's the total length of time?
21: The speaker spells out the name of the restaurant. Write the letters you hear.

Section 4

Read each text and put a cross (✗) by the missing word or phrase, as in the example.

Example:

> This playground is for under-fives only.
> Children must be accompanied by .... at all times.

A ☐ a friend
B ☒ an adult
C ☐ a brother or sister

22.

> All visitors must .... before entering
> the hospital wards to prevent disease.

A ☐ park their cars
B ☐ wash their hands
C ☐ buy flowers

23.

> Mr and Mrs William Brady request the company
> of Jane and Alex Kinsey on the occasion of their
> daughter's .... to James Norton.

A ☐ graduation
B ☐ marriage
C ☐ retirement

24.

> People with the following should not use this
> running machine:
> • high blood pressure
> • irregular heartbeat
> • ....
> • breathlessness

A ☐ a track suit
B ☐ running shoes
C ☐ muscular pain

25.

> **Buy our** .... **insurance now**
> **and get cover for:**
>
> - illness while abroad
> - flight cancellations
> - lost luggage
> - car breakdown
>
> *Buy online and save 10%*

A ☐ travel

B ☐ medical

C ☐ car

26.

> **Ticket Machine**
>
> ❯ SELECT DESTINATION
> ❯ ENTER DATE AND TIME OF TRAVEL
> ❯ CHECK AMOUNT TO PAY
> ❯ SELECT METHOD OF ....
> ❯ INSERT CARD OR CASH
> ❯ TAKE TICKET AND ANY CHANGE

A ☐ travel

B ☐ instruction

C ☐ payment

Tip strip

23: Which option can be followed by *to* + a person?
24: Pay attention to the other items in the list; they are all health problems.
25: What type of insurance would cover everything listed in the bullets?
26: You are buying a ticket. Think about the steps. What do you need to do after checking the cost of the ticket?

Section 5

Read the passage and answer the questions below. For each question, put a cross (✗) in the box next to the correct answer, as in the example.

A British man, Stuart McCoy, has just returned to Britain after cycling over 3,500 km for charity. His journey took him from London to Athens via Paris, Munich, Vienna and Belgrade. I interviewed him yesterday.

What made Stuart embark on such a long and arduous journey? "Well, I'm a student," he said. "I had nothing to do in the summer vacation, and badly needed exercise, but I also wanted to do something for others, and that's really what made me do it."

He first thought of raising money for an animal charity. Then after watching a TV programme, he decided half of the money would go to a children's charity. "But half way through my journey, there was a terrible earthquake in China and I immediately decided it would all go to Chinese earthquake victims."

How much did he raise? "Friends and relatives donated about £1,000 in all, and while I was travelling, generous people gave me another £500. But half of my total amount came from my university, which promised to double what I raised myself." So, in total £3,000 – not bad for four weeks cycling.

Not bad at all. So, did Stuart cycle back to London, too? "Of course, I did," he laughed. "No, I gave my bicycle to a children's charity in Greece and came back by train. My dad offered to buy me an air ticket, but I also believe in 'green' transport, so I decided against flying."

And Stuart's next journey? He smiled, "Well, I suppose it's possible."

Would he get a better bike or do it in a cooler season – spring, for example? "Well, my bike was fantastic and I'm only free in the summer, but I think I'd rather not go on my own next time."

Example: Where did Stuart finish his journey?

A ☒ Athens

B ☐ Paris

C ☐ Belgrade

27. What was Stuart's main reason for going on the journey?

A ☐ He wanted to help people.

B ☐ He needed exercise.

C ☐ He had nothing to do.

28. When did Stuart finally decide which charity to give money to?

A ☐ before the journey

B ☐ during the journey

C ☐ after the journey

29. Who was the most generous with donations?

A ☐ Stuart's university

B ☐ people Stuart met on the journey

C ☐ Stuart's friends and relatives

30. How did Stuart return home?

A ☐ by bicycle

B ☐ by plane

C ☐ by train

31. What would Stuart do if he did a similar journey in the future?

A ☐ get a better bike

B ☐ go with someone else

C ☐ go in the spring

Tip strip

27. Three reasons were mentioned for the journey Stuart made, but which phrase refers to the main reason?
29: What was the total donated? Think about the amounts that came from each of the three options.
30: What happened to his bicycle?
31: Look for a phrase which shows what he prefers to do "next time".

Section 6

Read the newspaper feature below and answer the questions.

Tip strip

32: What number will next month's event be? So, how many have already taken place?

33: Look for something different that is happening this year.

35: Something is mentioned especially for this.

THE RIVERSIDE VILLAGE OF UPTON is planning its tenth Summer Family Day to take place next month. All the usual activities will be there for families to enjoy and this time there will also be a talent show, "Upton Has Talent". Any parents, children or whole families who can sing, dance or generally entertain are welcome to take part. Interested? Then Mrs Bickley, the event organiser, would like to hear from you before 21st June on 0322 428111.

The Summer Family Day will be alongside the river, where there is going to be a special stage set up for "Upton Has Talent". Be there!

Example: Where is Upton located?

Beside a river

---

32. How many Summer Family Days has Upton had so far?

....

....

33. What is going to be new this year?

....

....

34. How should people contact Mrs Bickley?

....

....

35. What are the talent show participants going to perform on?

....

....

Tip strip

37: What is happening before the guests can chat together?
38: What is "The Peter Saunders Pavilion" replacing, and why?
39: What did he have to do unexpectedly?

LUDSDEN SCHOOL, fifty years old last month, is celebrating again. Next Wednesday sees the opening of the new sports pavilion, two years after building began on it. Head teacher, James Grey, has invited eighty guests, mostly former sports captains, to attend. After the Head's speech, guests will be able to chat together and reminisce, looking at old photographs of sports teams.

"The Peter Saunders Pavilion" will replace the one vandals burned down in 1985. "Sporty" Saunders, who retired from teaching through ill health last year, was hoping to attend on Wednesday, but has had to travel abroad unexpectedly.

Example: How old is Ludsden school?

50/fifty (years old)

36. When did work begin on the pavilion?

....

....

37. What is James Grey going to do first?

....

....

38. What happened to the old pavilion?

....

....

39. Why can't Peter Saunders attend the opening?

....

....

Section 7

Read the article below and complete the notes that follow, as in the example. Write **no more than three words** from the article in each gap.

Tips for Travellers Overseas

The first thing to do is check that your passport is valid. Holders of out-of-date passports are not allowed to travel overseas.

Then you can prepare for your trip. If you don't know the language, you can have all kinds of problems communicating with local people. Buying a pocket dictionary can make a difference. You'll be able to order food, buy things in shops and ask for directions. It's worth getting one.

There's nothing worse than arriving at your destination to find there are no hotels available. If you don't book in advance, you will end up spending precious time looking for accommodation when you are tired, finding yourself in less desirable areas or paying more than you should. Don't risk it!

Another frustrating thing that can happen is to go somewhere and not know about important sightseeing places. Get a guide book before you leave and make the most of your trip. It's a must.

Then, when you are ready to pack your clothes, make sure they are the right kind. It's no good packing sweaters and coats for a hot country or T-shirts and shorts for a cold one. Check the local climate before you leave.

Also, be careful how much you pack in your bags. It's easy to take too many clothes and then not have enough space for souvenirs. But make sure you pack essentials.

What about money? Well, it's a good idea to take some local currency with you, but not too much. There are conveniently located cash machines (ATMs) in most big cities, and it's usually cheaper to use them than change your cash in banks. Then you'll have more money to spend.

When you are at your destination, other travellers often have great information they are happy to share. Find out what they have to say. It could enhance your travelling experience.

Example: Make sure your passport is not *out-of-date*

---

40. Avoid problems communicating with local people by investing in a ....

41. It's advisable to reserve hotel rooms before you arrive at your destination to avoid staying in ....

....

42. To enjoy your trip as much as possible, buy a ....

43. Take clothes that suit the ....

44. Leave room in your bags for ....

45. Using ATMs to get local currency is convenient and ....

46. To get information talk to ....

Tip strip

40: What should you "invest in" by buying?

41: Find problems you might face if you don't book accommodation in advance.
45: Look for advantages of using ATMs.

46: Look for a source of information you can talk to at your destination.

Section 8

Use information from **Section 7** to help you write your answer.

47. You have just read an article giving tips to travellers overseas. Write an email giving travel advice to your friend in the United States, who is going to visit your country. Write **70–90** words and include the following information:

- how your friend could prepare
- suggest places to visit
- where to try traditional food

Use your own words.

Section 9

Tip strip

- Read both options very carefully before choosing one. Think: do you have some ideas and enough vocabulary to complete the task? For example, choose option B if you like writing articles and have recently seen or attended a sporting event.
- Think of the task type you have chosen. Is it an essay, an article, a letter to a magazine or an email? Remember what you have learnt about each task type. Both options here require you to write in paragraphs.
- Before you start writing, note down the main points you want to include in each paragraph. For A, you need to give different reasons, with examples, why friendship is important; for B, you need to give details of the sporting event (what, when and where it was, what happened, how you felt, etc).

  Back up your ideas with additional points; use simple and effective linking words or phrases.

  Remember to briefly summarise your opinion in the last paragraph.
- When you have finished, check that you have dealt with everything in the task prompt and that you have written 100–150 words.
- Finally, check your grammar and spelling.

48. Choose **one** of the topics below and write your answer in **100–150 words**.

Either:

A Write an essay on the following topic:

> The importance of friendship in the modern world.

Or:

B Write an article for your school magazine about a sporting event you saw recently and explain how you felt during the event.

Tip strip

- Think about the question the examiner asks and try to talk about it as much as you can. Try to provide reasons or talk about various aspects of the topic; don't wait for the examiner to use a follow-up prompt.

- You don't have to tell the truth if you don't want to! You will be marked on your language, not on your opinion. But, you do need to give specific information, so spend time thinking about your answer.

Prompt 1: Talk about a subject that you like at school. Explain why you like it and whether you enjoy doing its homework compared to other subjects, giving reasons.

Prompt 2: Describe what it is, say why it is important to you, who gave it to you, how long you have had it and where you keep it.

Prompt 3: Explain how you spend your free time, who you spend it with, where you usually go and what you do.

Prompt 4: Describe the book, say why you liked it, what made it interesting, if you liked the ending and whether you recommend it.

In this section you will speak on your own for about a minute. Your teacher/examiner will ask one of the main questions below and use the follow-up prompts if necessary.

Main prompt 1: *What subjects do you enjoy studying at school?*

Follow-up prompts:
- *Have you always enjoyed these subjects?*
- *Why is it that you prefer these subjects to others?*
- *How much homework do you get in your favourite subject?*
- *How would you feel if you had to do more homework?*

Main prompt 2: *What is your most valued possession?*

Follow-up prompts:
- *How long have you had it?*
- *When did you get it and who gave it to you?*
- *Why do you value this more than your other possessions?*
- *How would you feel if you lost it?*

Main prompt 3: *How do you usually spend your free time?*

Follow-up prompts:
- *Do you prefer to spend your free time with family or friends?*
- *What did you do last weekend?*
- *How do you think you'll spend your free time when you're older?*
- *If you had less homework, what would you do with your time?*

Main prompt 4: *What is the most interesting book you have ever read?*

Follow-up prompts:
- *What exactly made it interesting?*
- *Which of the characters did you like most?*
- *How did you feel at the end of the story?*
- *If you had the time, would you read more or do other things?*

Section 11 (2 minutes)

In this section you will discuss something with your teacher/examiner.
The question is:

> **"Is it better to shop in a shopping centre or to shop online?"**

What do you think?

Your teacher/examiner will use the following arguments to take an opposing view to yours.

For shopping centre:	• You can try things on.
	• You don't have to wait for your purchase.
	• It's a good way to do something with your friends.
	• If there's a problem with your purchase, it's easy to take it back.

For shopping online:	• You can visit many websites quickly.
	• They deliver your goods to your door.
	• You don't have to waste time walking around the shops.
	• You don't have to queue up to pay.

Tip strip
- Think about the question very carefully and decide which one you think is better and why. Explain your opinion giving reasons. You could say: *I think shopping online is better because you can save a lot of time by visiting different websites while sitting at home, rather than going to a shopping centre.*

- Whatever view you have, the examiner will take the opposing view. Remember this is a discussion, so it is important to listen to the examiner carefully, say if you agree or disagree and try to challenge him/her. For example, in answer to the comment above, the examiner might say: *But in a shopping centre you can try things on.* You could then say: *That's right, but when you shop online you can look for discounts and the best price quickly, and so get a better deal.*

In this section you will talk about this picture for up to 1 minute. Your teacher/examiner will say:

Now, here is a picture of inside a restaurant. Please tell me what you can see in the picture.

Tell your teacher/examiner what you can see in the picture.

Your teacher/examiner will now put this secondary prompt:

What is the mother of the two children doing and what do you think will happen next?

Tip strip

- Look at the picture very carefully and describe what you can see in it. You should talk about where the picture is set and what the general situation is, using the present simple tense. You could talk about who the different people are and what their relationships are.

- After you describe what you see, the examiner will ask you a question about the picture. Pay attention to the first part, *What is the mother of the two children doing …?* The question shows you can use both the present simple and the present continuous to describe the picture. The second part of the question … *what do you think will happen next?* asks you to react to the picture. Try to give reasons, for example, *I think the mother will ask the children to be quiet because … .*

- Try to link your sentences using linking words. This will help you to score higher marks for grammar, and the organisation of your ideas.

Section 13 (2 minutes)

In this section you will take part in a role play. Your teacher/examiner will explain the situation.

Test taker's card

You are in a restaurant. You are not happy with the food or the service, and want to complain. You have asked to see the manager.

- Explain the situation.
- Ask for a reduction in price.
- Come to an agreement with the manager.

Your teacher/examiner is the manager. Below is a sample script that your teacher/examiner may use.

You are in a restaurant. You have several things to complain about, especially the food and the service. You have asked to see the manager. I am the manager.

Ready? I'll start.

- *Good evening, sir. I understand there's a problem.*
- *I'm very sorry about that, sir. What exactly did you order?*
- *I'm afraid we can't reduce the price, but ...*
- *We can offer you a free dinner for two on ...*
- *Thank you, sir. We look forward to seeing you.*

That is the end of the test.

Tip strip
- Use the preparation time to think of some ideas you can use based on the test taker's card.
- Think of the relevant vocabulary in relation to the topic so that you can speak without hesitation when you start. For example, *complain, the quality of the food, expect*.
- When you read the test taker's card, take note of the role the examiner is playing so you know how to react. For example, here, the examiner is the manager and a person in authority, so the interaction must be polite even though you want to make a complaint.

adverse (adj) not good or favourable; that makes it difficult for something to happen

arduous (adj) involving a lot of strength or effort

appointment (n) an arrangement for a meeting at an agreed time and place, for a particular purpose

ATM (n) Automated Teller Machine – a machine outside a bank that you use to get money from your account

available (adj) able to be used or can easily be bought or found

blood pressure (n) the force with which blood travels through your body

book (v) to make arrangements to stay in a place, eat in a restaurant, go to a theatre, etc., in the future

breakdown (n) an occasion when a car or a piece of machinery breaks and stops working

breathless (adj) having difficulty breathing because you are very tired, excited or frightened

briefcase (n) a flat case used especially by business people for carrying papers or documents

burn down (phr v) if a building burns down or is burned down, it is destroyed by fire

cancellation (n) a decision that an event that was planned will not happen; a decision to end an agreement or arrangement that you have with someone

cash machine (n) a machine in or outside a bank, supermarket, or other public building from which you can obtain money with a special plastic card

chat (v) to talk in a friendly, informal way, especially about things that are not important

cover (n) the protection insurance gives you, so that it pays you money if you are injured, something is stolen, etc.

currency (n) the system or type of money that a country uses

donate (v) to give something, often money, to a person or an organisation in order to help them

double (v) to make something twice as big or twice as much

earthquake (n) a sudden shaking of the Earth's surface that often causes a lot of damage

embark on (phr v) to start something, especially something new, difficult or exciting

enhance (v) to improve something

favour (n) something that you do for someone in order to help them or be kind to them

fit (adj) someone who is fit is strong and healthy, especially because they exercise regularly

fit (v) if a piece of clothing fits you, it is the right size for your body

fitness (n) when you are healthy and strong enough to do hard work or play sports

foot passenger (n) a passenger on a ship who has not brought a car with them

footbridge (n) a narrow bridge used only by people who are walking

frustrating (adj) making you feel annoyed, upset or impatient because you cannot control a situation or achieve something

graduation (n) the time when you complete a university degree course or your education at an American high school

heartbeat (n) the action or sound of your heart as it pumps blood through your body

homework (n) work that a student at school is asked to do at home

look after (phr v) to take care of someone by helping them, giving them what they need, or keeping them safe

manage (v) to succeed in doing something difficult, especially after trying very hard

never mind (phr) a phrase used to tell someone not to worry or be upset about something

pack (v) to put things into cases, bags, etc., ready for a trip somewhere

painkiller (n) a medicine which removes or reduces pain

platform (n) the raised place beside a railway track where you get on and off a train in a station

postpone (v) to change the date or time of a planned event or action to a later one

raise (v) to collect money that you can use to do a particular job or help people; to improve the quality or standards of something

regret (v) to feel sorry about something you have done and wish you had not done it

reminisce (v) to talk or think about pleasant events in your past

replacement (n) someone or something that is used to replace another person or thing

resume (v) to start doing something again after stopping or being interrupted

retirement (n) when you stop working, usually because of your age; the period after you have stopped work

riverside (adj) along the edges of a river

run (v) to organise or be in charge of an activity, business, organisation or country

set up (phr v) to start a company, organisation, committee, etc.

sightseeing (n) when you visit famous or interesting places, especially as tourists

speech (n) a talk, especially a formal one about a particular subject, given to a group of people

suit (v) clothes, colours, etc. that suit you, make you look attractive

suspend (v) to officially stop something from continuing, especially for a short time

take off (phr v) if a plane takes off, it rises into the air from the ground

terminate (v) if a train, bus or ship terminates at a particular place, its journey ends there

tournament (n) a competition in which players compete against each other in a series of games until there is one winner

trainers (n pl) shoes that you wear for sports or as informal clothing

valid (adj) a valid ticket, document or agreement is legally or officially acceptable

vandal (n) someone who deliberately damages things, especially public property

ward (n) a large room in a hospital where people who need medical treatment stay

would rather (v) used to say that you would prefer to do or have something

Practice Test 2

Section 1

You will have 10 seconds to read each question and the corresponding options. Then listen to the recording. After the recording you will have 10 seconds to choose the correct option. Put a cross (✗) in the box next to the correct answer, as in the example.

Example: What is the speaker's job?

A ☐ a hotel manager
B ☒ a bus driver
C ☐ a rail passenger

1. What are the speakers discussing?

   A ☐ health problems
   B ☐ travel insurance
   C ☐ hotel cancellations

2. What is the woman doing?

   A ☐ offering accommodation
   B ☐ arranging a hotel
   C ☐ suggesting a trip

3. What does the speaker think of the hotel?

   A ☐ It's nice.
   B ☐ It's disappointing.
   C ☐ It's uncomfortable.

4. Who is the man speaking to?

   A ☐ a librarian
   B ☐ a shop assistant
   C ☐ a policewoman

5. What are the speakers discussing?

   A ☐ a family meal
   B ☐ a robbery
   C ☐ money

6. What is next to the post office?

A ☐ a bakery

B ☐ a supermarket

C ☐ a bank

7. What is the speaker's job?

A ☐ a photographer

B ☐ a shop assistant

C ☐ a guide

8. What is the relationship between the speakers?

A ☐ They are brothers.

B ☐ They are old friends.

C ☐ They are colleagues.

9. Who is speaking to Angie?

A ☐ Angie's sister

B ☐ Angie's mum

C ☐ Angie's teacher

10. Where is Danny?

A ☐ at customer service

B ☐ in the car park

C ☐ outside the main entrance

Section 2

11. You will hear a recording about a police station. Listen to the whole recording once. Then you will hear the recording again with pauses for you to write down what you hear.
Make sure you spell the words correctly.

Section 3

12–16 You will hear a conversation. First, read the notes below, then listen and complete the notes with information from the conversation. You will hear the recording twice.

Example: Name of agency: _Cameron Holidays_

12. Contact telephone number: ....

13. Type of family holiday: ....

14. Length of holiday: ....

15. Preferred accommodation: ....

16. Special requirements: ....

17–21 You will hear a recorded message. First, read the notes below, then listen and complete the notes with information from the recorded message. You will hear the recording twice.

Example: Message from Raj to: _Jamie_

17. New date for wedding: ....

18. Reason for change: ....

19. Location of hotel: ....

20. Jamie's accommodation: ....

21. Jamie to call Raj after: ....

Section 4

Read each text and put a cross (**X**) by the missing word or phrase, as in the example.

Example:

> If you would like to have .... in your room, tick what you want on the menu and hand it to reception the night before. It is served between 7 a.m. and 9 a.m.

A   **X**   breakfast

B   ☐   lunch

C   ☐   dinner

22.

> PROTECT YOUR SKIN
> - Wear a hat
> - Put on a ....
> - Use sun block
> - Don't stay in the sun too long

A   ☐   swimsuit

B   ☐   sunglasses

C   ☐   T-shirt

23.

> ### Would you like a language exchange ....?
> If you want to learn Chinese and learn about Chinese culture, and can help me with my English, email me.
> *jennywang@fastmail.com*

A   ☐   student

B   ☐   partner

C   ☐   course

24.

> **The following are not permitted inside the stadium:**
> - glass bottles
> - ....
> - video cameras
> - pets

A ☐ flags

B ☐ spectators

C ☐ dogs

25.

> Join **Cadham** .... now and:
> - borrow books
> - rent CDs
> - enjoy free Internet access
>
> *Located between the cinema and the sports centre.*

A ☐ sports centre

B ☐ film club

C ☐ library

26.

> **STUDENT ADVICE CENTRE**
>
> Do you need help organising your .... ,
> finding accommodation or dealing with money?
> *If so, come and speak to our experts.*
> *It's free and confidential.*

A ☐ time

B ☐ room

C ☐ finances

Section 5

Read the passage and answer the questions below. For each question, put a cross (✗) in the box next to the correct answer, as in the example.

A FAMILY BEACH HOLIDAY almost turned into a nightmare yesterday when eight-year-old Jason Bligh fell almost four metres from a tree onto rocks, not far from Pebble Beach in Australia.

Jason's parents were swimming at the time and too far away to see what had happened. Fortunately, Jason's friend, Maggie Young, was with him and she ran to tell her mother. She called the emergency services on her mobile and then ran into the water to tell Jason's parents.

A quarter of an hour later, a helicopter arrived to take Jason to hospital. Jason was still unconscious. So, after carefully putting him onto a stretcher, the paramedics lifted him into the helicopter which flew him to Stanley hospital – a journey of ten minutes. His parents joined him half an hour later after driving to the hospital in their car.

In the helicopter, Jason regained consciousness and wondered where he was, but he felt OK. When he had an examination at the hospital, the doctor could not believe Jason had no broken bones. As expected, he had cuts and bruises on various parts of his body, but nothing more serious than that.

When Jason's parents arrived at the hospital, they were relieved that he was not badly injured. The doctor told them Jason could go to the beach again after two days in bed. "Yes, but next time at the beach he's going to stay with us all the time," laughed Linda, his mother. "And no more climbing!"

Jason remembers nothing about his fall. And he can't remember much about the helicopter ride. "But I remember hearing Maggie asking me if I was alright," he says. "She was fantastic. She'll be my friend forever."

Example: What was Jason doing when he fell?

A ☐ rock climbing
B ☒ climbing a tree
C ☐ playing on the beach

27. Who saw what happened to Jason?

A ☐ Jason's parents

B ☐ Jason's friend, Maggie

C ☐ Maggie's mother

28. How long did it take the helicopter to get to Jason?

A ☐ 10 minutes

B ☐ 15 minutes

C ☐ 30 minutes

29. What surprised the doctor when she examined Jason?

A ☐ He had bruises on his body.

B ☐ There were cuts on his body.

C ☐ Nothing was broken.

30. What advice did the doctor give?

A ☐ Jason should have some rest.

B ☐ Jason should not climb.

C ☐ Jason should stay with his parents at the beach.

31. What can Jason remember most about the incident?

A ☐ the helicopter ride

B ☐ his fall

C ☐ Maggie's voice

Read the newspaper feature below and answer the questions.

Marriage Can Last

GEORGE AND MOLLY BRADFORD have been married for seventy years. Molly remembers their days at Harven Primary School, where they first met, with fondness. "It wasn't love at first sight, but we always had fun together," she says. When they were twenty, they did fall in love, but the Second World War had just started and they decided to wait to get married. Fifty years later, in 1995, they went on a cruise, paid for by their children, to celebrate. And now, in 2015, they are as happy as ever. "I have no regrets," says George. "I just wish I could do it all again."

Example: How long have George and Molly been married?

(for) 70 years

32. Where did George and Molly get to know each other?

....

33. What prevented George and Molly from getting married at twenty?

....

34. How did George and Molly spend their fiftieth anniversary?

....

35. What would George do if he had the chance?

....

Read the newspaper article below and answer the questions.

HILLSIDE MARKET has been in Longley for a hundred years. But all that might change soon.

Developers, Smith and Brown, have applied to build a new shopping centre where the market is. If the application is successful, building will begin early next year.

Angry local residents have formed an action group, SOM (Save Our Market), and plan a series of demonstrations before the final decision on the market's future next month.

John Frain, a stallholder for thirty years, says, "They tried this ten years ago and it failed. It's going to fail again."

Example: Where is Hillside Market?

In Longley

36. What might replace the market?

37. What exactly is "Save Our Market"?

38. When will people find out about the market's future?

39. How long ago did John Frain start working at the market?

Read the article below and complete the notes that follow, as in the example. Write **no more than three words** from the article in each gap.

When tourists decide on a holiday destination, they tend to think of well-known places such as Paris, Rome, Rio, New York or Bangkok. But perhaps there are other less well-known places which are also worth visiting, perhaps your home town or village, or your local area in general.

There may be more to see in your local area than you think. It's sometimes just a question of finding it, which is not always easy.

For example, in my home town, Harford, there's a fantastic museum where you can follow the five-hundred-year history of the town as a port. It's located in a small riverside building that used to be a fisherman's cottage in the past but has been a museum since the last fisherman moved out fifty years ago.

Hardly any visitors come to the museum, which is a shame, but at least that means you have the place to yourself. You can spend many hours looking at the old photographs and talking to the man who works there, Harry. Harry is one of the most interesting people you'll ever meet. He knows absolutely everything about the town's history.

So what is there in your local area? Maybe a fantastic restaurant that only a few people outside your area know about. Restaurants for local people are often much better value than more famous ones. If you spend less money in restaurants, you have more to spend on other things.

Why not email us and tell us about your local area? Include a brief description of some of the places to see. Readers' emails will be in next week's edition.

Example: Tourists usually go to _well-known places_

40. Less popular places can be ....

41. In your local area it can be difficult to find things ....

42. Harford has a long history ....

43. Until fifty years ago the museum was ....

44. The museum doesn't attract many ....

45. You often spend less money in restaurants ....

46. Next week's edition will include ....

Section 8

Use information from **Section 7** to help you write your answer.

47. You have just read a magazine article encouraging people to write about places of interest in their own areas. Now write an email to the editor about a less well-known place in your area. Write **70–90 words** and include the following information:

- give information about the place
- explain why this place is special
- say what visitors can do there

Use your own words.

48. Choose **one** of the topics below and write your answer in **100–150 words**.

Either:

A Write an essay on the following topic:

> Why is it important to protect historic buildings?

Or:

B Write an article for your school magazine about a special relationship you have with someone.
  – How is it special?
  – How do you think the relationship will develop in the future?

Section 10 (1.5 minutes)

In this section you will speak on your own for about a minute. Your teacher/examiner will ask one of the main questions below and use the follow-up prompts if necessary.

Main prompt 1: *Tell me about one of the teachers who works at your school.*

Follow-up prompts:
- *What do you like or dislike about him/her?*
- *How long has he/she been at your school?*
- *What subjects does he/she teach?*
- *How do you imagine he/she spends his/her free time?*

Main prompt 2: *What was your favourite possession when you were very young?*

Follow-up prompts:
- *Why did you like it so much?*
- *How long did you have it?*
- *Who bought it for you and why?*
- *When you have children in the future, will you get them one of these?*

Main prompt 3: *What is the most interesting hobby you have ever had?*

Follow-up prompts:
- *How old were you when you started it?*
- *Do you still do it or have you given it up?*
- *Why did you decide to take it up?*
- *What hobbies have other people in your family got?*

Main prompt 4: *Tell me about a film you have seen recently.*

Follow-up prompts:
- *Did you see it at the cinema or on television?*
- *What did you think of the film?*
- *How did the film make you feel?*
- *If you had the chance, would you watch it again?*

Section 11 (2 minutes)

In this section you will discuss something with your teacher/examiner.
The question is:

"Is it better to eat at home or in a restaurant?"

What do you think?

Your teacher/examiner will use the following arguments to take an opposing view to yours.

For home:	• You can eat exactly what and how much you want at home.
	• You know what's in the food.
	• It's cheaper and usually tastes better.
	• If there's too much, you can save it for the next day.

For restaurants:	• The atmosphere is better.
	• There's no washing-up to do.
	• You can try food you don't usually eat.
	• It's a good place to meet your friends.

Section 12 (1.5 minutes)

In this section you will talk about a picture for up to 1 minute. Your teacher/examiner will say:
Now, here is a picture of a wedding reception. Please tell me what you can see in the picture.
Tell your teacher/examiner what you can see in the picture.

Your teacher/examiner will now put this secondary prompt:
How do you think the young man and the old woman are feeling? Why?

Section 13 (2 minutes)

In this section you will take part in a role play. Your teacher/examiner will explain the situation.

> ## Test taker's card
>
> One of your friends has invited you to his/her birthday party. You have already got plans for that day and cannot go. You phone your friend and explain the situation.
>
> - Explain the situation.
> - Decline the invitation.
> - Offer to try and change your plans.
> - Suggest meeting your friend for dinner soon.

Your teacher/examiner is your friend. Below is a sample script that your teacher/examiner may use.

Your friend has invited you to his/her birthday party. You have already got plans for that day and cannot go. You are phoning your friend. I am your friend.

Ready? I'll start.

- *Hi. How are you? Are you coming to my party?*
- *Oh, no. You have to come to the party. Can't you change your plans?*
- *Thanks. Try to come. It'll be great.*
- *That's a good idea. Where do you think we should go?*
- *OK. Let me know if you can come to my party.*

That is the end of the test.

accommodation (n) a place for someone to stay, live or work

belongings (n pl) the things that you own, especially things that you can carry with you

break (n) a short holiday

bruise (n) a purple or brown mark on your skin that you get because you have fallen, been hit, etc.

cancel (v) to say that an event that was planned will not happen

clean up (phr v) to make a place completely clean and tidy

colleague (n) someone you work with, used especially by professional people

conscious (adj) awake and able to understand what is happening around you

customer service (n) the part of a company or business that deals with questions, problems, etc., that customers have

emergency services (n pl) official organisations such as the police or the fire service that deal with crime, fires and injuries

fall in love (phr v) to develop a strong feeling of attraction for someone

fine (n) money that you have to pay as a punishment

fisherman (n) someone who catches fish as a sport or as a job

fondness (n) a strong feeling of affection for someone, especially someone you have known for a long time

get married (phr v) become the husband or wife of someone

gift shop (n) a shop that sells small things that are suitable for giving as presents

graffiti (n) rude, humorous or political writing and pictures on the walls of buildings, trains, etc.

hobby (n) an activity that you enjoy doing in your free time

incident (n) an event, especially one that is unusual, important or violent

jewellery (n) small things that you wear for decoration, such as rings or necklaces

librarian (n) someone who works in a library

locate (v) to find the exact position of something

mobile (phone) (n) a telephone that you can carry with you and use in any place

nightmare (n) a very frightening dream

package holiday (n) a holiday organised by a company at a fixed price that includes the cost of travel, hotel, etc.

paramedic (n) someone who has been trained to help people who are hurt or to do medical work, but who is not a doctor or nurse

prevent (v) to stop something from happening, or stop someone from doing something

rent (v) to regularly pay money to live in a house or room that belongs to someone else or to use something that belongs to someone else

requirements (n pl) something that someone needs or asks for; something that must be done because of a law or rule

a shame (n) used to say that something is a cause for feeling sad or disappointed

stallholder (n) someone who rents or keeps a table or a small shop in a market

stretcher (n) a type of bed used to carry someone who is too ill or injured to walk

succeed (v) to do what you tried or wanted to do

sun block (n) cream or oil that you rub into your skin, in order to stop the sun's light from burning you

tick (n) a mark written next to an answer, something on a list, etc., to show that it is correct or has been dealt with

Exam Guide

Section 1: 3-option multiple choice

What is being tested?

Section 1 tests your ability to understand the main idea of a short spoken text.

What do you have to do?

Answer ten questions. For each question, you will listen to a short recording with one or two speakers. You will hear each recording once. For each one, you will see a question and three possible answers (A, B and C). You have to listen and decide which answer is the best.

Strategy

- Read and listen to the instructions.
- For each question, you will have 10 seconds to read the question and the options. Read them carefully and highlight the key words. Think about what is different in each option.
- Listen carefully – you will hear each conversation only once.
- Put a cross in the box next to the answer you think is best.
- The questions are marked as either correct or incorrect. If you are not sure, choose the answer you think is most likely – you may be right.

Preparation tips

- Try to get used to hearing a range of voices and accents. Search online for an English language radio program on a topic that interests you. You won't understand every word, but listen and try to get the key ideas as you listen.
- Practise reading and listening at the same time. When you are doing practice tests, try to follow the words on the question paper as you listen to the instructions. Practise highlighting the key words in the paper and predicting the topic before you listen to the recording.

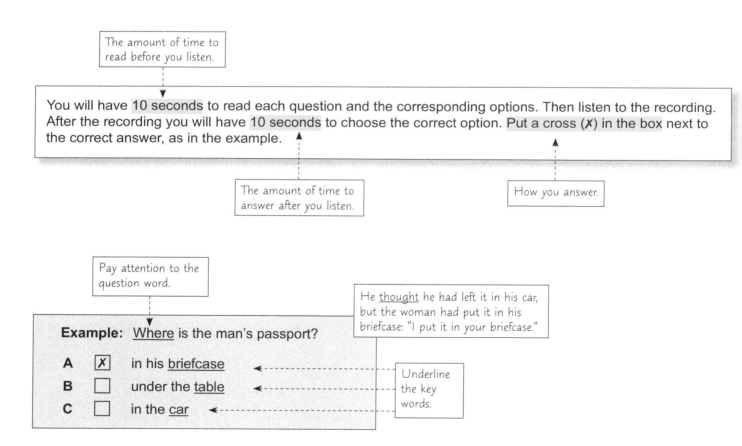

The amount of time to read before you listen.

You will have 10 seconds to read each question and the corresponding options. Then listen to the recording. After the recording you will have 10 seconds to choose the correct option. Put a cross (✗) in the box next to the correct answer, as in the example.

The amount of time to answer after you listen.

How you answer.

Pay attention to the question word.

He <u>thought</u> he had left it in his car, but the woman had put it in his briefcase: "I put it in your briefcase."

Example: <u>Where</u> is the man's passport?

A [✗] in his <u>briefcase</u>

B [ ] under the <u>table</u>

C [ ] in the <u>car</u>

Underline the key words.

Section 2: Dictation

What is being tested?

Section 2 assesses listening and writing skills. It tests your ability to understand an extended piece of speech by transcribing a spoken text.

What do you have to do?

Listen to one person speaking and write exactly what you hear with correct spellings. You will hear the recording twice; the second time with pauses, giving you time to write down word-for-word what you hear. There is one dictation to complete and therefore only one recording.

Strategy

- Read and listen to the instructions.
- Pay attention to the topic of the recording.
- During the first reading of the dictation, listen very carefully to the whole recording. The subject is always given in the instructions. Try to understand the overall extract and pick out some key words. If you write the key words as you hear them, you will have a better chance of recognising the topic vocabulary and identifying words that go together.
- You will hear the recording for a second time. The second time, it is with pauses giving you time to write the words down.
- If you miss or misunderstand a word during the second listening, leave a space and keep writing. When the dictation has finished, read it through and use your knowledge of topic vocabulary and grammar to help you guess the missing word(s).
- Check you have spelt the words correctly.

Preparation tips

- Improve your general listening skills: practise listening to a topic and understanding the main ideas. Search online for an English language radio program on a topic that interests you:
  - You won't understand every word, but listen and try to note down the key words as you listen.
  - Practise picking out the keywords; these are usually words that the speaker stresses.
  - Listen again and try to write down as much as you can. Practise listening and writing down the key words at the same time.
  - Check what you have written. Use your knowledge of grammar to get word endings right.

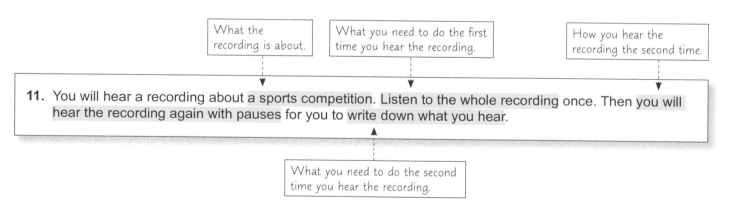

What the recording is about.

What you need to do the first time you hear the recording.

How you hear the recording the second time.

11. You will hear a recording about a sports competition. Listen to the whole recording once. Then you will hear the recording again with pauses for you to write down what you hear.

What you need to do the second time you hear the recording.

Section 3: Text, note completion

What is being tested?

Section 3 tests your ability to extract specific information from extended spoken texts.

What do you have to do?

Listen to two recordings, either a monologue or dialogue, and complete notes for each using the information you have heard. There are ten gaps to complete; five per recording. You will hear each recording twice.

Strategy

- Read and listen to the instructions.
- You will hear two recordings. For each recording you will have five questions to answer. For each recording you will have 30 seconds to read the questions. Read them carefully and highlight the key words. See what kind of information is missing.
- Listen carefully. Try to keep track of the questions as you listen to the recording. Use the key words that you have highlighted in each question to help you with this. You can expect to hear some of the key words in the recording.
- Try to make notes while you listen to the recording.
- Listen to the recording for a second time. Then read the questions again and try to complete the sentences /notes that you did not complete the first time and check your answers.
- If you are completing a sentence, check that your answer makes sense and it is grammatically correct.

Preparation tips

- Improve your general listening skills. Search online for an English language radio program on a topic that interests you. You won't understand every word, but listen and try to note down the key words as you listen.
- When you are doing practice tests, work on predicting the missing information:
  - Read the notes and use the words before and after each gap to predict the missing words.
  - Turn statements into questions. This will help you to see what kind of information is missing.
  - Predict meaning by looking at content words (words that carry meaning) in the sentence. For example, if the sentence is: *You can join a class in a gym or ....* . The words "in a gym or" suggest that the missing word is a place that is similar to a gym.
  - Use your knowledge of grammar to predict what part of speech is needed.

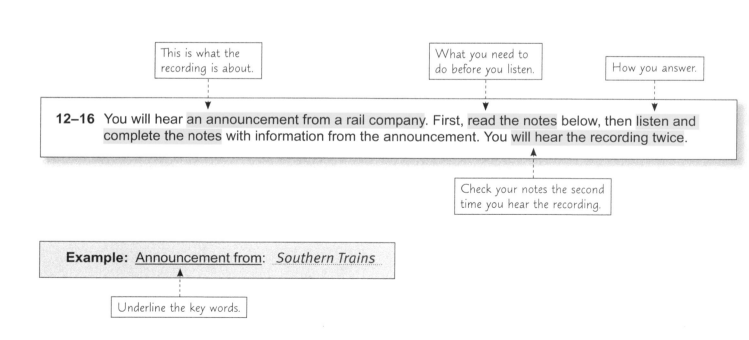

This is what the recording is about.

What you need to do before you listen.

How you answer.

12–16 You will hear an announcement from a rail company. First, read the notes below, then listen and complete the notes with information from the announcement. You will hear the recording twice.

Check your notes the second time you hear the recording.

Example: Announcement from: *Southern Trains*

Underline the key words.

Section 4: Gap fill 3-option multiple choice

What is being tested?

Section 4 tests your ability to understand the purpose, structure and main idea of short written texts.

What do you have to do?

Answer five questions. Read five short texts, each containing a gap, and choose which one out of three answer options is the missing word or phrase. There are five gaps to complete, one per text.

Strategy

- Read the instructions carefully.
- Read each question and the three options carefully and highlight any key words. Think about what is different in each option.
- When you have chosen your answer, check the other options again to make sure they cannot be correct.
- Re-read the text with your selected option inserted in the gap to check that the text makes sense (in terms of meaning). If it doesn't, you will need to review the option you chose.

Preparation tips

- Do as many practice tests as possible so that you fully understand the task and what you should do.
- Learn how to analyse texts; ask yourself questions such as why the text was written, what type of text it is and what the writer's purpose is.
- Practise highlighting the keys words in the text and using this information to consider the meaning of the missing words. You can practise this by working with a partner: choose one text each, remove some words from the text, and then swap them. Highlight the keywords and try to understand what information is missing.
- Keep a vocabulary notebook in which you write down useful vocabulary you come across, arranged by topic.
- Try to learn words in chunks. When you learn a new word, write down not only the word, but also the sentence it is used in.

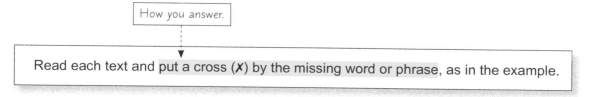

How you answer.

Read each text and put a cross (✗) by the missing word or phrase, as in the example.

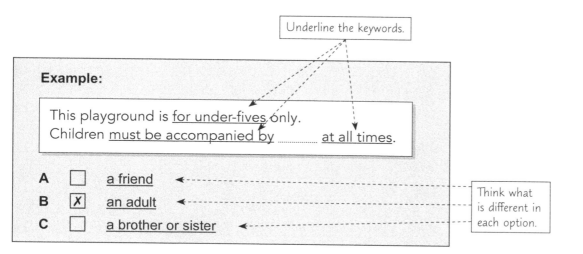

Underline the keywords.

Example:

This playground is <u>for under-fives</u> only.
Children <u>must be accompanied by</u> .... <u>at all times</u>.

A ☐ <u>a friend</u>

B ☒ <u>an adult</u>

C ☐ <u>a brother or sister</u>

Think what is different in each option.

Section 5: 3-option multiple choice

What is being tested?

Section 5 tests your ability to understand the main ideas in an extended written text.

What do you have to do?

Read a text and answer five questions (or complete five sentences) from a choice of three answer options. There are five answers to choose and one text.

Strategy

- Before you read the text, read the multiple-choice questions and underline the key words in the prompt. These words will tell you what information you need to find in the text. You could try to find the answer in the text before looking at the choices. If you then find that one of the options is close to your answer, you can be more confident that it is correct.

- Read the text and use the key words to find the right place for the answer in the text.

- Read around the key words to understand the information so you can answer the question correctly.

- Sometimes the options are a paraphrase of the ideas in the text. You need to read the relevant part of the text carefully to understand the whole idea and to match it to the correct option.

Preparation tips

- Do as many practice tests as possible so that you fully understand the task and what you should do.

- Read as much as you can. The reading that you do outside the classroom will help you become a better reader.

- Practise understanding the information in a text by reading around key words.

- Learn to scan a text. This is reading a text quickly to look for a specific piece of information without reading everything.

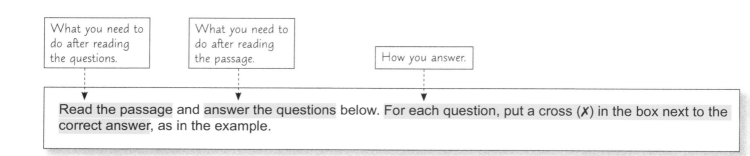

What you need to do after reading the questions.

What you need to do after reading the passage.

How you answer.

Read the passage and answer the questions below. For each question, put a cross (✗) in the box next to the correct answer, as in the example.

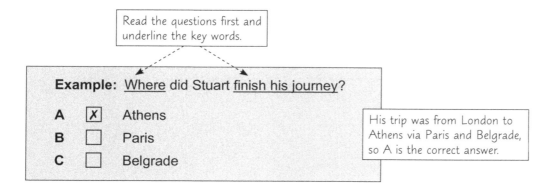

Read the questions first and underline the key words.

Example: Where did Stuart finish his journey?

A	✗	Athens
B	☐	Paris
C	☐	Belgrade

His trip was from London to Athens via Paris and Belgrade, so A is the correct answer.

Section 6: Open-ended question

What is being tested?
Section 6 tests your ability to understand the main points of short written texts.

What do you have to do?
Read two texts and answer eight questions about them using single words or short answers. There are eight questions to answer; four per text.

- Before you read the text, read the questions and focus on the key words in the questions. These are often question words such as *what, why, how, when* and words that carry meaning such as nouns and verbs.
- Pay attention to the key words, they will tell you exactly what information you need to find in order to produce a short, accurate answer.
- Try to answer each question briefly and accurately using words from the text where appropriate.
- Try to avoid writing long answers with unnecessary words. Your answer doesn't have to be written as a sentence – often a word or phrase is enough.
- To help you focus your thoughts, underline or highlight the area in the text where you think the answer is.

- Do as many practice tests as possible so that you fully understand the task and what you should do.
- Remember that Pearson Test of English General aims to test real-life skills. The reading that you do outside the classroom will help you become a better reader.
- Practise reading texts quickly all the way through to understand the main ideas. You can read articles in newspapers, magazines or online and summarise the main ideas or opinions in them, even if you don't know all the vocabulary.
- When you're doing practice tests, focus on the key words in the questions. These are often words such as *what, why, when* and *how*. These words will tell you exactly what information you need to find to give a short and accurate answer. Practise giving short and accurate answers to questions. This will help you to avoid using unnecessary words when providing an answer.

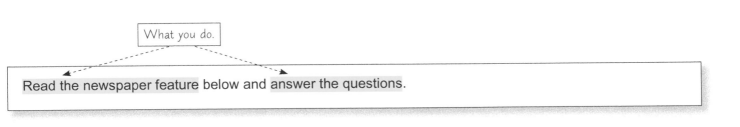

What you do.

Read the newspaper feature below and answer the questions.

Underline the question words before you read the text. Here, the question word tells you the answer is a place/location.

Example: <u>Where</u> is Upton located?

Beside a river

Section 7: Text, note completion

What is being tested?
Section 7 tests your ability to extract specific information from an extended written text.

What do you have to do?
Read a text and use information from it to fill gaps in seven incomplete sentences or notes. You must use no more than three words from the text to do this. There are seven sentences or notes to complete and one source text.

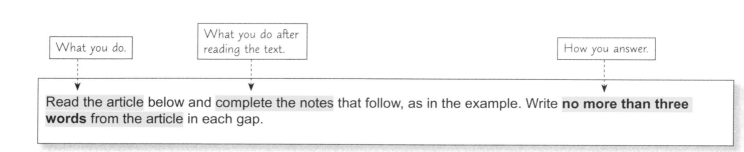

What you do.

What you do after reading the text.

How you answer.

Read the article below and complete the notes that follow, as in the example. Write **no more than three words** from the article in each gap.

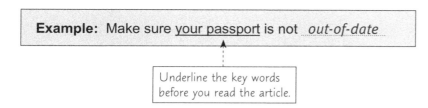

Example: Make sure <u>your passport</u> is not *out-of-date*

Underline the key words before you read the article.

Section 8: Write correspondence

What is being tested?

Section 8 tests your ability to write a piece of correspondence.

What do you have to do?

Write an email or a formal or information letter based on information given in Section 7. There is one text to write (70–90 words). There is a "tolerated" word limit of 56–99 words for Section 8. If the response is below or over this limit, you will automatically score 0 for the section.

Strategy

- Read the instructions very carefully.
- Focus on the task requirements. Correspondence is a form of communication that has a "reader". Check the task instructions to find out what you are writing and who you are writing to. You need to understand the purpose of the correspondence.
- Cover all the bullet points in your writing. Avoid writing too much about one and not enough about the others.
- Highlight the parts of the text in Section 7 that you could use to plan the content of your answer. You will need to refer to the text in Section 7, usually by summarising the main idea and/or commenting on it. In either case, you should use your own words as far as possible. The *Writing Guide* on pages 55–59 provides some help with this.
- Leave a few minutes at the end of the task to check through your work.
- Check your writing for the accuracy of your grammar and spelling.

Preparation tips

- Work on improving your vocabulary by reading and noting down words and expressions you might use to write on topics such as family, hobbies, interests, work, travel and current events.
- Learn how to plan your writing and what information you need to include. Practise using markers and linking words. Use the *Writing Guide* on pages 55–59, which also gives you useful language you can use.
- Understand what kind of mistakes you make in your writing; try to improve these areas. Build a list of your errors (for example, using past work marked by your teacher) as a guide.
- Practise checking through your work for spelling and punctuation errors. Work with a partner to discuss content and organisation, and to correct each other's language errors.

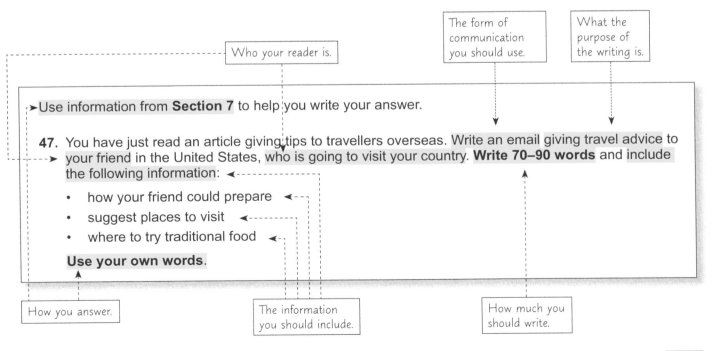

Who your reader is.

The form of communication you should use.

What the purpose of the writing is.

►Use information from **Section 7** to help you write your answer.

47. You have just read an article giving tips to travellers overseas. Write an email giving travel advice to your friend in the United States, who is going to visit your country. **Write 70–90 words** and include the following information: ◄

- how your friend could prepare ◄
- suggest places to visit ◄
- where to try traditional food ◄

Use your own words.

How you answer.

The information you should include.

How much you should write.

Section 9: Write text

What is being tested?

Section 9 tests your ability to write a short text from your own experience, knowledge or imagination.

What do you have to do?

Write a piece of free writing from a choice of two given topics. The form of the response may be factual (blog entry, article, instructions), critical (review, report, essay) or analytical (essay, analysis of an issue or argument, explanation). There is one text to write (100–150 words). There is a "tolerated" word limit of 60–165 words for Section 9. If the response is below or over this limit, you will automatically score 0 for the section.

Strategy

- Read the introduction to the task and the prompts, and choose one topic.
- Use the prompt to decide what type of text you need to write and choose the correct format (for example, an article) and style (for example, semi-formal) for the task.
- Highlight all the key words in the prompt so you know what you need to cover. Use this information to organise your answer.
- Sometimes it is easier to answer a question than it is to write about a statement. Rewrite the prompt as a question to make it clearer.
- Use as wide a range of words, linking words and phrases to link your sentences and paragraphs, as you can, along with a range of grammatical structures and different tenses.
- Leave a few minutes at the end of the task to check through your work.

- Check that the style you have used is appropriate. Have you communicated your ideas clearly? Would the reader understand your arguments?
- Check that your grammar and spelling are correct.

Preparation tips

- Look at examples of articles, reviews, reports and letters in English language newspapers and magazines. How are they organised? What makes them interesting to read? Use the *Writing Guide* on pages 55–59 to help you.
- Practise developing an argument for or against an idea, giving your opinions and backing them up with a few reasons.
- Practise writing an essay or article and keeping to the required number of words.
- Work with a partner to discuss content and organisation, and to correct each other's language errors.

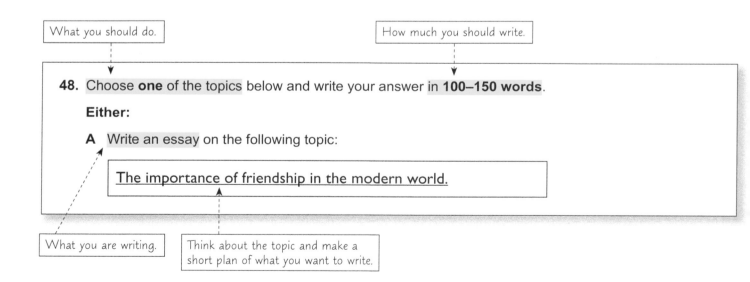

What you should do.

How much you should write.

48. Choose **one** of the topics below and write your answer in **100–150 words**.

   Either:

   A Write an essay on the following topic:

   The importance of friendship in the modern world.

What you are writing.

Think about the topic and make a short plan of what you want to write.

Section 10: Sustained monologue

What is being tested?

Section 10 tests your ability to speak continuously about matters of personal information and interest.

What do you have to do?

Speak continuously about matters of personal information and interest for up to one minute. The examiner might ask you some follow-up questions to encourage you to continue talking. The questions focus on regular and routine activities, past activities and experiences, future plans, tastes and preferences. This section of the test lasts 1.5 minutes.

Strategy

- You need to talk about a familiar topic on your own for about one minute.
- If you don't speak for very long, the examiner may ask you some questions to encourage you to talk. Listen to the examiner's questions very carefully before giving an answer.
- Try to give a reason and provide an answer which is more than just a few words.
- Provide reasons using a range of grammatical structures and vocabulary in order to show your language ability.
- Don't try and learn pieces of language by heart before your interview. It won't sound natural and the learned language will probably be irrelevant to the subject you are speaking about.

Preparation tips

- Make sure you are familiar with the task: what the examiner will do and how long the section lasts.
- Practise talking about yourself with other students on a range of different topics. Choose a topic, for example, school, and ask each other different questions.
- Practise talking for about one minute on a topic, with a classmate timing you.
- Work on building your vocabulary on a range of familiar topics.
- Practise listening carefully to questions and thinking about the topic before giving an answer.

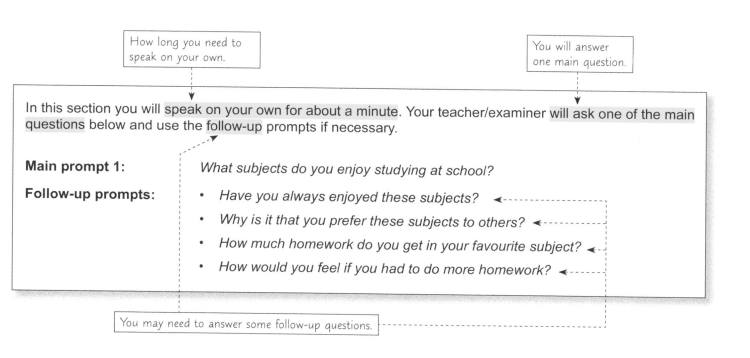

How long you need to speak on your own.

You will answer one main question.

In this section you will speak on your own for about a minute. Your teacher/examiner will ask one of the main questions below and use the follow-up prompts if necessary.

Main prompt 1: *What subjects do you enjoy studying at school?*

Follow-up prompts:
- *Have you always enjoyed these subjects?*
- *Why is it that you prefer these subjects to others?*
- *How much homework do you get in your favourite subject?*
- *How would you feel if you had to do more homework?*

You may need to answer some follow-up questions.

Section 11: Discussion

What is being tested?

Section 11 tests your ability to discuss a concrete issue.

What do you have to do?

Give and support your opinion on a topic in response to a question that the examiner asks you. This section of the test lasts 2 minutes.

Strategy

- Listen carefully to the examiner in order to understand the focus of the question.
- Think critically about the topic. Try to provide a relevant answer using appropriate structures and language functions.

Preparation tips

- Make sure you are familiar with the structure of the task: what you are expected to do, what the examiner will say, and how long the task is.
- Practise asking for and giving your opinions on current events. When answering a question, always expand on your views.
- Practise agreeing or disagreeing with a point.
- Practise paraphrasing. This is expressing the same idea in different ways. This will be useful if you cannot remember a word or expression.
- Practise evaluating what is being said by others in a discussion. Think about what they say in relation to the topic of the discussion.

- Learn a range of phrases that you can use to express your opinion, agree or disagree, such as:

Expressing your opinion

Well, in my opinion … / if you ask me… / I'd say that … / I think …

I don't believe that …

Agreeing/disagreeing

That's a very good point, but don't you think …

As you said, … However, …

I'm afraid I don't agree. I believe that …

I take your point, but I still think …

That's an interesting point, but we also need to consider …

You could be right.

The way I see it, …

Interrupting politely

I'm sorry, but …

Sorry to interrupt, but …

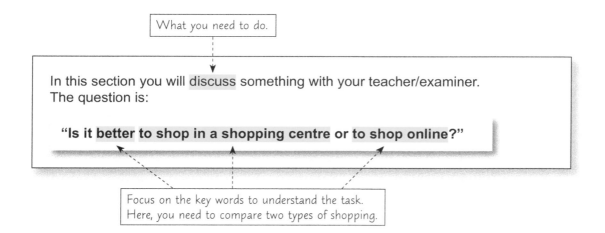

What you need to do.

In this section you will discuss something with your teacher/examiner. The question is:

"Is it better to shop in a shopping centre or to shop online?"

Focus on the key words to understand the task. Here, you need to compare two types of shopping.

Section 12: Describe picture

What is being tested?

Section 12 tests your ability to speak continuously about a picture and interpret some aspect of it.

What do you have to do?

Speak continuously about a picture that the examiner presents to you for about 45 seconds. Then answer the follow-up question that the examiner asks you. This section of the test lasts 1.5 minutes.

- You have to talk about a picture for just under one minute.
- The examiner will present you with a card and will ask you to describe a picture.
- Talk about different aspects of the picture: where it is, who is in it, what you think is happening. Describe any people or notable objects, how the people look, and so on. Show your knowledge of vocabulary and grammar.
- After you describe what you see in the picture, the examiner will ask you a question.
- Listen carefully to the question and give your opinion.
- Use linking words to give and support your opinion.

- Make sure you are familiar with the task: what you are expected to do, what materials you will be given, what the examiner will say and how long the task is.

- Practise describing a picture and talking about it for about one minute with other students: use pictures on a range of topics and ask each other questions. Practise using some of the phrases below:

What is in the picture

In the picture I can see …

This is a picture of … / This picture shows …

There's / There are… / There isn't a … / There aren't any …

What is happening

The man is …-ing

The people are …-ing

Where in the picture

At the top/bottom of the picture …

In the middle of the picture … / On the left/right …

Next to / in front of / behind/near/under …

Making assumptions

It looks like a … / She looks like … / He might be …

It might be a … / Maybe it's a …

He could be …-ing

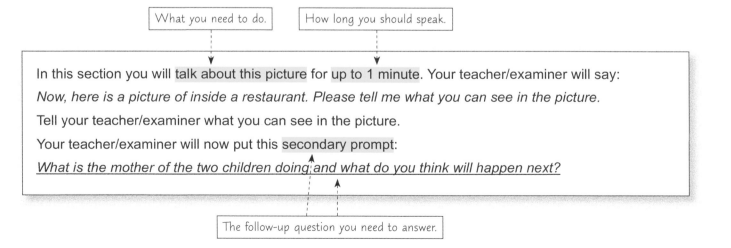

What you need to do.

How long you should speak.

In this section you will talk about this picture for up to 1 minute. Your teacher/examiner will say:

Now, here is a picture of inside a restaurant. Please tell me what you can see in the picture.

Tell your teacher/examiner what you can see in the picture.

Your teacher/examiner will now put this secondary prompt:

What is the mother of the two children doing and what do you think will happen next?

The follow-up question you need to answer.

Section 13: Role play

What is being tested?

Section 13 tests your ability to perform and respond to language functions appropriately.

What do you have to do?

Take part in a role play with the examiner, using a role card with information and instructions. This section of the test lasts 2 minutes.

What you need to do.

In this section you will take part in a role play. Your teacher/examiner will explain the situation.

What your role is; what you are doing.

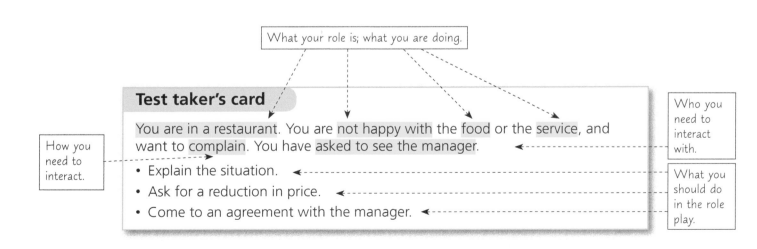

Test taker's card

You are in a restaurant. You are not happy with the food or the service, and want to complain. You have asked to see the manager.

- Explain the situation.
- Ask for a reduction in price.
- Come to an agreement with the manager.

How you need to interact.

Who you need to interact with.

What you should do in the role play.

Writing Guide

Introduction

Writing tasks in Pearson Test of English General

In Pearson Test of English General, there are two sections to assess your writing skills.

Section 8

In Section 8 you are asked to write a piece of correspondence. This may be a letter, an email or another form of electronic communication, such as a contribution to a web page.

What you have to write will always be a response to the text you have read in Section 7. For example, you may be asked to respond to a newspaper story by writing a letter to the newspaper. You will need to refer to the text in the previous section, usually by summarising the main idea and/or commenting on it. In either case, you should use your own words as far as possible, not simply copy parts of the original text. You will probably also need to say how the ideas in the text relate to your own opinions or experience. Exactly what you need to include is indicated by the bullet points in the instructions.

The word limit in this section is **70–90 words.** This is quite a small number, so it is important that you don't waste words.

Section 9

This section is a free writing task in which you will need to draw on your own experience to describe, analyse, explain, give an opinion about or express reasons for something. What you are asked to write can take various forms. It may be something factual (for example, a blog entry or article) or something critical or analytical (for example, an essay, review or report).

There will be a choice of two tasks. The topics will be related to two of the themes of the test, so there may be ideas you can use in other sections, but, again, you should use your own words. The word limit is **100–150 words**.

General advice

There are specific tips in the *Exam Guide* section of this book. Below are some more general pieces of advice relating to writing in general and in Pearson Test of English General.

- Always be aware of the reader, the person or people that you are writing for. This will have an effect on both the content (what you write) and the style (how you write). Generally speaking, an informal style (similar to what you would use when speaking) is best for letters and emails to friends, and for light-hearted articles, while a semi-formal or neutral style is better for more serious articles or essays. It is very unlikely that you will have to write something in a very formal style.

- Show the examiner what you know, not what you don't know. If you're not sure how to say something in English, either say it in a different way or say something else.

- Before you do the test, don't try to learn large sections and long phrases, for example, introductions, and try to fit them into your writing, whatever the topic. This often looks unnatural and is usually easy for the examiner to notice. It is often a waste of words as well: if you use a lot of words on "decoration", you might find you don't have enough words to get your real message across.

- Make a short plan of what you want to write. In this way, your writing will be clearer and better organised. Use paragraphs to organise your writing. The text should be divided into three parts: an introduction, the body of the text and a conclusion. Linking words and phrases will also help you do this, but, if the writing is well organised, it is probably enough to have two or three basic words or phrases for various purposes. For example, use *and*, *also* and *in addition* to add extra information or *but*, *whereas* and *however* to show contrast. The most important thing is that you understand how to use them.

- When you have finished writing, check what you have written for mistakes, especially "silly" mistakes – the kind you make under pressure. Try to be aware of the kinds of mistake you tend to make frequently.

- Your writing will be marked for how well it performs the task as well as for the language, so make sure you cover all the points required by the question and bullet points.

Letters to magazines or newspapers

Model answer

You have read a review of a new CD in High Notes, a music magazine. Write a letter to the magazine explaining your opinion of the review. Write **70–90 words** and include the following information:

- say what you think of the review
- explain your opinion
- suggest what readers should do

Use your own words.

Start by saying why you are writing. This first sentence is a very useful way of beginning most formal or neutral letters because you can simply replace the verb *complain* with another one that explains what you want to do, for example, *enquire/ask (about), tell/inform/explain* or *give my opinion.*

Use this word to introduce the first of two or more points you want to make (in this letter there are only two).

This phrase, and other more formal ones, like *In summary, To sum up* and *In conclusion*, should be used to summarise what you have already stated or suggested.

Dear *High Notes,*

I want to complain about your review of Lilly Aspen's new CD, "Dreams".

Firstly, there are mistakes in the review. For example, you say there are only three new songs, but there are five. More importantly, however, the review suggests that few fans will not like the CD. That's wrong! Everyone I talk to thinks it is great.

In short, your readers should ignore what you say. "Dreams" is Lilly's best CD in years.

Yours faithfully,

[79 words]

In "real life", there are rules or conventions about how to address the person or magazine you are writing to, but in PTE General only the main body of what you write is assessed.

But is a useful way to contrast two things in the same sentence. Often, simple connectors like *but, and* or *so* are all you need to state a point clearly and effectively.

This phrase shows that you are moving on to your main point. It is often more effective to make your less important points first and keep the main point till last.

As with opening salutations, there are rules about "signing off", but these are not assessed in PTE General.

Formal opening
Dear Sir/Madam

Reason for writing
I recently read about … and would like to …
I am writing in reply/response to your article …
I am writing to complain about …
I was very disappointed with …
I would like to learn/know more about …

Introducing a point
Firstly, … / My first suggestion is … / I would like to suggest …
Secondly,/I further suggest …
Another possibility is …
Not only … but also …

Formal closing
Yours faithfully, (if you don't know the name of your addressee)
Yours sincerely, (if the name is given in the task)

Emails and other forms of electronic communication

Model answer

You read a posting on a website about pet dogs being a nuisance to the public. Now write an email to the website expressing your opinion. Write **70–90 words** and include the following information:

- what you think of the posting
- a suggestion for what people should do
- how you feel about the subject

Use your own words.

At the beginning of any kind of correspondence, always ask yourself what the reader needs to know, for example, who you are, why you are writing or what you are writing about. In this context, all of these things are already clear, so you can get straight to the point.

When arguing a point, it is an effective strategy to concede (partially accept) a point from the opposite argument before making your own point. Useful words/phrases for introducing this kind of concession include *Obviously* and, as here, *Of course.*

I disagree with Paul Drake's bad opinion of dogs. Of course, dogs can be annoying or dangerous if their owners do not control them. However, we can easily solve these problems through proper training of dogs and their owners.

After conceding a point, state your own argument, linking it to the previous statement with words like *though* or *however* (if it's a new sentence) or *but* (if it's in the same sentence).

In this kind of correspondence, there is no need to introduce your opinion with phrases like *In my opinion* or *From my point of view.* It is understood that the whole point of what you are writing is to give your opinion, so using phrases like this is simply a waste of words.

The main point is dogs bring great benefits. Dogs improve the health of their owners because they provide natural opportunities for exercise. Dogs also guard homes and protect owners. Most importantly, dogs offer their owners a friend and companion for life. Is it any wonder, then, that dog owners are happier and live longer than other people?

When presenting a point of view for or against something, it is important to give clear and effective reasons to support your views.

The word total of 96 words is over the maximum number; the instructions ask you to write 70–90 words. If your answer is a few words too long or short, there won't be any penalty. Your teacher will be able to give you more information on the "tolerated" word limits.

[96 words]

This is called a rhetorical question. It is asked to make a point rather than find out information, so it doesn't expect an answer. Questions like this are typical in spoken arguments and they can also be used in written contexts like this because the style here is quite informal.

Useful language

Opening statements

I have just read your article on … and I feel I must …
You raised some issues that I feel strongly about …
I am completely in agreement.

Expressing and supporting opinions

It is possible that …
In general …, however …
I believe/do not believe that … because …
It is clear that …
It is important to remember that …

Listing arguments

Firstly, … / To begin with, …
Secondly, … / Another point to remember is …
Finally, … / In conclusion, …

Essays

Model answer

Write an essay in answer to the following question.

> What are the advantages and disadvantages of learning English in your own country?

Write **100–150 words**.

Don't waste words at the beginning of your response. Go straight into your main points.

It is cheeper to learn English in your own country because you can live at home and continue to study at school or go to work. This is the main advantage. Another advantage is that you won't miss your family or friends. Also, you will be in your normal surroundings so you will be relaxed and comfortable.

Back up your idea with additional points, using simple and effective linking words or phrases rather than more formal ones like *Moreover.*

This phrase introduces the contrast with the first paragraph. It is especially useful when discussing advantages and disadvantages. It isn't necessary to have used *On the one hand* for the previous point.

On the other hand, if you study English in America or Britain, you will also learn about the culture in addition to the language. You will use English in everyday situations and have daily contact with native speakers with different accents, whereas at home you might not have many chances to practise your English outside the classroom.

This shows you are adding an additional, contrasting point to the same sentence to list other advantages of studying English in an English-speaking country.

Write a concluding paragraph that summarises the question and expresses your own opinion.

Nowadays, with the Internet, you can communicate in English more easily from your own country. On balance, I think it is better to study English in your own country.

This is a useful way to introduce your opinion when there are arguments for and against a particular point of view.

[143 words]

Useful language

Opening phrases
Nowadays …
These days, it seems that …

Making points
Many people feel that …
Another argument in favour is …
It is clear that …
This means that …
According to …

Contrasting points
On the other hand …
Other people think …
I personally feel that …

Organising and linking ideas
First of all, …/ Secondly, …/ In addition, …
Moreover, … / Furthermore, …
So, …/ As a result, … / Therefore, …
However, … / On the one hand, … / On the other hand, …
Finally, … / To summarise, … / In conclusion, …

Summarising
All in all, I think …
To sum up, I believe that …

Articles

Model answer

You see this advertisement in an English language magazine and decide to write an article to enter the competition.

Summer Competition

Write an article about healthy eating. We'll publish the best 5.

Great Prizes!!!!!

Write **100–150 words**.

The first sentence is important to attract the reader's attention. You can do this in different ways, such as stating the topic quickly, simply and clearly, asking the reader a direct question or giving an interesting quotation.

Articles usually have a title or a heading to attract the reader's attention. Including one will make your article look more realistic.

A balance is what you need!

Nowadays, many young people eat food which is not healthy. We all love junk food but we can have too much of it. The key to a better diet is balance. According to experts, we should eat at least five portions of fruit and vegetables a day to balance unhealthy food like burgers and fries. This will help us to avoid health problems such as heart disease. Fruit and vegetables are quite low in calories and there is so much variety to choose from. If you don't like apples, have a banana instead! Simple! So, enjoy your burger, but maybe once a week, not every day.

My top tips for a balanced diet are:

- Remember the five a day rule.
- Cut out or cut down on unhealthy foods.
- Have three good meals a day.
- Snack on fruit, not on chocolate.
- Exercise to use up calories.
- Enjoy your food!

[154 words]

The writer is putting himself or herself in the same position as the readers to try and get the message of the article across.

Where possible, include brief and relevant examples. These strengthen the arguments you are making.

The style of writing here is quite informal or even quite conversational. This is common in articles which often address the reader personally, but it depends on the subject and where the article will be printed.

Unlike other pieces of writing, articles often contain headings, sub-headings, lists or bullet points.

It is important to decide what the aim of your article is, for example, to explain, to advise, to persuade, to inform or to entertain. From the title of this article, the purpose is to persuade readers as well as inform them. The organisation and the style of the article try to reinforce these purposes.

Useful language

Introductory/rhetorical questions

Have you ever ...? /
Did you know ...?
What would you do if ...?
What would life be like if ...?
What do you think about ...?

Expressing opinion

It is clear that ...
It is important to remember that ...
This means that ...

Giving examples from personal experience

Personally, I prefer to ...
I can say this from experience ...

Introducing first point

The first thing to consider is ...
First of all, ... / Firstly, ... / To begin with ...

Introducing more points

Another consideration is / Another thing to consider is ...
In addition to this ... / Apart from that ...

Audioscript

Practice Test 1

Section 1

Narrator: You will have 10 seconds to read each question and the corresponding options. Then listen to the recording. After the recording you will have 10 seconds to choose the correct option. Put a cross (✗) in the box next to the correct answer, as in the example.

Example

Listen to the conversation. Where is the man's passport?

Man: I can't find my passport. I thought I left it in the car.

Woman: No, I put it in your briefcase. It's on the table in the kitchen.

Narrator: The correct answer is A.

Number 1

Listen to the telephone conversation. What is Mandy doing?

Mandy: Hi, Jan. Mandy here.

Jan: Hi, Mandy.

Mandy: Thanks for inviting me and Steve to dinner on Saturday. Unfortunately, Steve's working on Saturday, so we won't be able to come. Really sorry about that.

Jan: Never mind. We can do it another time.

Narrator: **Number 2**

Listen to the conversation. Why is the speaker buying a card for his friend?

Man: Hello, I need a card for a friend.

Shop assistant: A birthday card?

Man: No, she did me a big favour the other day so …

Shop assistant: So, you want a "Thank You" card. Look, here's a nice one – pink with flowers on it. I'm sure she'll like it.

Narrator: **Number 3**

Listen to the telephone conversation. What is the relationship between Margaret and Pat?

Pat: Hi, Margaret.

Margaret: Hi, Pat.

Pat: About Dad's surprise birthday party. It's going to be at his friend Tom's house. And I've sent invitation cards to all our cousins, so you don't need to do that.

Margaret: Thanks, Pat.

Narrator: **Number 4**

Listen to the telephone conversation. What is the speaker's dad going to do?

Woman: Hi, Dad. Mary here. Are you busy this morning?

Man: Not really, Mary. Why?

Woman: Well, I've got a dental appointment and Alex can't go to school.

Man: Has she still got a cold?

Woman: Yes. Can you look after her until twelve?

Man: Sure. No problem.

Narrator: **Number 5**

Listen to the announcement. Where is the speaker?

Man: Your attention please. We are sorry to announce that the 8.48 service to London has been cancelled. The next train to London will leave from platform 6 in approximately 10 minutes. Can passengers for London please make their way over the footbridge to platform 6.

Narrator: **Number 6**

Listen to the conversation. Where are the speakers?

Travel agent: I'd recommend the 10 a.m. flight, Sir. It is £50 more, but it arrives much earlier.

Man: OK. I'll book that. I want to arrive in time for lunch.

Travel agent: And will you need transport to the airport?

Man: No, thanks. My wife'll drive me there.

Narrator: **Number 7**

Listen to the conversation. What kind of transport are the speakers talking about?

Man 1: And how much does it cost?

Man 2: Nothing. Bikes and foot passengers travel free. You just get on board and five minutes later you're the other side of the river. From there, there's a bus to town.

Number 8

Listen to the conversation. Who is talking to Mr Smith?

Doctor: Well, Mr Smith, it seems you've broken your toe.

Man: When can I play football again?

Doctor: Not for three months. You need rest. And if you continue to feel pain, buy some painkillers from the chemist's.

Narrator: **Number 9**

Listen to the conversation. What is the woman looking for?

Woman: Oh, is it that building near the church?

Man: Yes, that's right. The sports centre is just past the supermarket and opposite the church. It's in this street. You can't miss it.

Narrator: **Number 10**

Listen to the conversation. What does the boy want?

Boy: They're too small, Mum. I can't get them on.

Mother: OK. Let's look for a bigger pair. Ah, look, there are some over there next to the football shirts.

Boy: Mum, they're trainers! I can't wear them to play football.

Section 2

Narrator: **Number 11**

You will hear a recording about a sports competition. Listen to the whole recording once. Then you will hear the recording again with pauses for you to write down what you hear. Make sure you spell the words correctly.

Man: The inter-schools football tournament, postponed in February due to weather conditions, is going to be held in May. Eight teams, organised into two groups, will play group games. The winners will meet in the final.

Narrator: Now listen again and write down your answer.

Man: The inter-schools football tournament, / postponed in February / due to weather conditions, / is going to be held in May. / Eight teams, organised into two groups, / will play group games. / The winners will meet in the final.

Section 3

Narrator: **Numbers 12 to 16**

You will hear an announcement from a rail company. First, read the notes below, then listen and complete the notes with information from the announcement. You will hear the recording twice.

Woman: Attention please. This is a passenger service announcement from Southern Trains. Southern Trains regrets to announce that train services to London have been suspended and trains will now terminate at New Bridge. Passengers will need to leave their train at New Bridge and take the replacement bus service to London. The replacement buses will be waiting for you outside New Bridge station.

This problem is due to a minor incident on the main line near New Bridge. Engineers are now dealing with the situation and we expect it to take 2 hours before normal service resumes. All other Southern Trains services are running normally.

If you need more information during the day, please visit our website and click on "Information". Once again, we are sorry for any inconvenience.

Narrator: Now, listen again.

Numbers 17 to 21

You will hear a recorded message. First, read the notes below, then listen and complete the notes with information from the recorded message. You will hear the recording twice.

Woman: Hi, Janet. Melinda here. I've got some really exciting news. You won't be able to guess, so I'll tell you. You know our son, Colin? The one living in Australia? Well, he's coming to England. Not for a holiday or anything like that – it's a business trip – but he has to work in London, so he's going to stay with us. Well, with us for a week and then with some friends for another week before he goes back home. And guess what! He's coming next month!

Anyway, I was thinking of having a welcome home party for him. He's arriving on the 15th of June – that's a Thursday – so I thought the 17th of June would be a good idea. I'm going to book a table at that new restaurant in town. I think it's called "Rivarera" – anyway, it's spelled R-I-V-I-E-R-A. Write it in your diary – we'd love you to come.

Call me when you get in.

Bye.

Narrator: Now, listen again.

That is the end of the listening section of the test. Now, go on to the other sections of the test.

Practice Test 2

Section 1

Narrator: You will have 10 seconds to read each question and the corresponding options. Then listen to the recording. After the recording you will have 10 seconds to choose the correct option. Put a cross (✗) in the box next to the correct answer, as in the example.

Example

Listen to the announcement. What is the speaker's job?

Man: We are just about to arrive at the King's Hotel. If you booked your holiday through a travel agent, this is your hotel. Would passengers going to the railway station please stay on the bus.

Narrator: The correct answer is B.

Number 1

Listen to the conversation. What are the speakers discussing?

Man: So, what exactly will it cover?

Woman: Well, if you are ill or have an accident, we will pay the costs for that.

Man: What about flight or hotel cancellations?

Woman: Yes, that's also included. And if you lose money or belongings, that's covered, too.

Narrator: **Number 2**

Listen to the telephone conversation. What is the woman doing?

Woman: Mike, I've heard you and Jan are going on a trip to Paris.

Man: That's right. I'm going to arrange a hotel soon.

Woman: No, don't do that. I've got an apartment in Paris. You can stay there.

Man: Really? That's great. Thanks.

Narrator: **Number 3**

Listen to the telephone conversation. What does the speaker think of the hotel?

Man: How's the hotel? Is it nice?

Woman: Not really. It's quite comfortable, but not as good as I had imagined. In the brochure it looks much nicer.

Man: Yeah, they always look nice in brochures.

Narrator: **Number 4**

Listen to the conversation. Who is the man speaking to?

Man:	Can I return these books, please? Here's my card.
Librarian:	I'm afraid they're a week late.
Man:	Yes, I know. Sorry. How much is the fine?
Narrator:	**Number 5**
	Listen to the conversation. What are the speakers discussing?
Man:	It happened last night while I was at a restaurant with my family.
Policeman:	And what's missing, sir?
Man:	They took my computer and some of my wife's jewellery. Fortunately, I had my money and cards with me.
Policeman:	OK. Please fill in this form.
Narrator:	**Number 6**
	Listen to the conversation. What is next to the post office?
Man:	Is it very far?
Woman:	No. Walk along this road until you come to a bank. Turn left there and keep going for another hundred metres. The post office is between a bakery and a butcher's. If you see the supermarket, you've gone too far.
Narrator:	**Number 7**
	Listen to the announcement. What is the speaker's job?
Man:	Please remember that photography and filming are not allowed anywhere in the museum. However, guide books with pictures are on sale in the gift shop. Now, please follow me into the first hall.
Narrator:	**Number 8**
	Listen to the telephone conversation. What is the relationship between the speakers?
Man 1:	John, what a surprise! I haven't seen you for years.
Man 2:	No, I just got back from China. I saw your brother yesterday and got your number.
Man 1:	Great! Let's meet up. I'm going out with colleagues tonight. How about tomorrow?
Narrator:	**Number 9**
	Listen to the conversation. Who is speaking to Angie?
Schoolgirl:	Did you want to see me, Miss?
Teacher:	Yes, Angie. There's a test on Friday, so don't forget to do your homework. Your mum can help you with it. Oh, and tell your sister about the test, too.
Schoolgirl:	OK, Miss.

Narrator:	**Number 10**
	Listen to the announcement. Where is Danny?
Woman:	This is an announcement for the parents of seven-year-old Danny Thorpe. Danny was found in the car park ten minutes ago and is now waiting for you at the customer service desk just inside the main entrance of the supermarket. Thank you.

Section 2

Narrator:	**Number 11**
	You will hear a recording about a police station. Listen to the whole recording once. Then you will hear the recording again with pauses for you to write down what you hear. Make sure you spell the words correctly.
Newsreader:	The new police station in the city centre, which opened only two months ago, has become the latest victim of graffiti artists. The clean up could cost up to about £50,000 of local taxpayers' money.
Narrator:	Now listen again and write down your answer.
Newsreader:	The new police station in the city centre, / which opened only two months ago, / has become the latest victim / of graffiti artists. / The clean up / could cost up to about £50,000 / of local taxpayers' money.

Section 3

Narrator: **Numbers 12 to 16**

You will hear a conversation. First, read the notes below, then listen and complete the notes with information from the conversation. You will hear the recording twice.

Travel Agent: Cameron Holidays. Julie speaking. Can I take your name and contact details?

Mark: Mark Roberts and my phone number is 01323 441235.

Travel Agent: Thank you, Mr Roberts. How can I help?

Mark: Well, I need information for a family holiday.

Travel Agent: A summer holiday? A city break?

Mark: No. We've never been skiing and we want to try that.

Travel Agent: I see. When are you planning to go?

Mark: In March, ideally, for about four days.

Travel Agent: Usually, package holidays are for whole weeks. Is that too long?

Mark: No, that's fine. Let's say a week.

Travel Agent: And do you want a hotel or bed and breakfast?

Mark: Actually, we'd rather have an apartment.

Travel Agent: Mm. Apartments are difficult to find in March. Would a hotel be OK if we can't find an apartment?

Mark: Sure.

Travel Agent: OK, Mr Roberts. Leave it with me and I'll call you back.

Mark: Oh, one more thing. We might rent a car, so car parking at our accommodation would be good.

Travel Agent: No problem, Mr Roberts.

Narrator: Now, listen again.

Numbers 17 to 21

You will hear a recorded message. First, read the notes below, then listen and complete the notes with information from the recorded message. You will hear the recording twice.

Man: Hi, Jamie. Raj here. I've got some important news for you. Sonal and I have had to change the date of our wedding to the 23rd of July. Sorry about that. You'll remember it was originally on the 25th of June – well, we really didn't have any choice but to change it because I'm going to be away on business until the end of June.

The good news is the location is going to be the same – The King's Head Hotel in Ightham. That's I-G-H-T-H-A-M if you want to look it up on the internet. Some of the guests will be staying at the hotel, but don't worry about accommodation for yourself – you can stay at my flat of course.

Anyway, I'm really sorry about the change, Jamie – I hope you can still come. Call me between nine and eleven tonight and we can have a chat. Bye.

Narrator: Now, listen again.

That is the end of the listening section of the test. Now, go on to the other sections of the test.